Telling the Truth

Caitlyn Gehl

Copyright © 2024 Caitlyn Gehl
All rights reserved
First Edition

PAGE PUBLISHING
Conneaut Lake, PA

First originally published by Page Publishing 2024

Disclaimer: this book contains talk of self-harm and sexual assault. Nothing is in extreme detail but read at your own discretion.

ISBN 979-8-89157-247-8 (pbk)
ISBN 979-8-89157-261-4 (digital)

Printed in the United States of America

You'll always be the words in my stories

Brokenness isn't always beautiful
This nearly killed me

Don't say you love me out of convenience
Don't say you love me because you feel sorry for me
Don't waste the strongest words just to make me feel good
Don't waste your breath
Don't waste the energy
And most of all
Don't waste my hope
Actions speak louder than words ever will
So you don't love me
You don't adore me
You don't mean it
You may not love me
But I know for a fact
I love you with everything in me
I can't change you
And I accept that
But at least don't lie
Tell the truth
You don't love me

I healed because I learned
I grew because I changed
I lived because I fought

Darling, take your time
No need to rush what you want to last forever

You only tell me you love me when you wrap your hands around my waist
Or when your fingers slip up my thighs
You only call me beautiful as you grab my chest without consent
Or when you suck on my skin as I struggle to breathe
My body aches with guilt
As I try to push you away
You only appreciate me when you overpower my body and mind
My people-pleasing tendencies cause my innocent body to be overtaken by your masculinity
I'm scared
I don't like this
And I'm out of control over something that will change my life forever
I hate this,
But I can't say no
I can't be weak
I hold my ground as your tongue slips into my throat
Your hand holds the back of my neck,
Making it so I can't lean back
I'm afraid
I'm powerless
And I am *never* going to be the same

My shadow pulls me back the later the day gets
The longer my shadow grows
It becomes heavier
Making me drag my feet
They used to be astonishing to my innocence
A little friend that was always there, even if you couldn't see it
Now it's a friend you rarely see
But like then, it's always there
You don't want to look back to see it
My inner child needs healing
But a Band-Aid won't fix this
This isn't a scraped knee from the sidewalk
Or a paper cut from a coloring sheet
It needs cleansing
Not the cleaning like washing chalk off your hands
Or cleaning dirt from under your fingernails as you dug for worms
If I could go back in time
Treat a little girl like she should be, I would
Let's do it all over again
Restart the tape
Change the plot
But I can't
I can't change my past
And I'm paying that price now
I struggle to not take the blame
If I wasn't me
Would things have been different?
Maybe not
Or maybe so
I'll never know
I must accept that
And know things won't change

But maybe one day they will
And nothing will be the same

I lost the thing I needed most
But you found the thing you wanted
When I wished under the stars that night
I just hoped I wasn't forgotten

It's hard to let go when the memories never fade

I wonder how different everything would have been if I wasn't the way I am

I'm drowning but I don't have the energy to swim

If only you knew how much I suffered when you left

I'm falling but you're still not here to catch me

Under the waves of words I'm not speaking, I'm drowning

Maybe if you felt the words you said, things would be different

A smile hides the hours of tears that have now dried on my cheeks
A broken heart bandaged up by weak Band-Aids
Quickly snapped by pretty little lies
But she's so put together, right?
She's so independent, right?
The hours of sobbing on the cold bathroom floor are hidden by
    a quickly closed door
I feel my hands quiver as I put on my mask, waiting for the day
    that I show that happiness does not last

We live to love
We learn to love
We love to love
Love is love until it's lost
But if you're *truly* in love, can you fall out?
Can you love someone forever?
Love can be false
Take your hand, guiding you, forcing you to believe it was love
It was true love,
You knew it, right?
It was true until it wasn't
I knew I loved to love
But I didn't know someone could lie to love
My spark was gone
But you took my lighter and lit it
You tried to blow it out plenty of times
But my love for you stayed
It stayed no matter how hard your blows were
The flame swayed left, right, right on the brink of extinguishing
It stayed for so long
Love lives for so long
Until one day the blow is enough
The light stops,
It's dark
Ignite it
Do it,
But it won't work
The flame won't come back
It won't burn bright
My love for you stayed but my hatred for you grew
So yeah,
You can love someone even if they don't love you
You blew out my flame

You took my light and strength
You took me
Love was born
Love lived
But loved died
You killed love
You killed me

You're like an old song I still love. New songs come and go, after bursts of addiction and admiration for them. Someday, the old song comes on the radio, and I crank it up to max volume. The windows are down, and I am screaming every word. After the song is over, I am reminded of what an amazing song it is. My love for that song never changes. The new songs didn't make me forget the lyrics. I'll forever love that song, even if it is not on a recent replay. And I will forever love you.

I wish people understood that I can love them without *loving* them

It hurts to love,
Especially when what you love hurts you

Don't worry
We still dance in the kitchen
You're just a ghost now

You were a good liar
But I still fell in love with your words

I never knew love could die
Just as quickly as it was born

When you think of love,
Do you think about me?

I would have never left
If you didn't leave first
And that,
That's scary

I can't regret meeting you
I just regret how I let you hurt me

If things could be different
I would have left earlier

You repeatedly hurt me
But I forced myself to believe that you made me happy

I believed you loved me
I was wearing the rose-colored glasses

I hope you never treat anyone else
The way you treated me

You made me believe
I deserved to be treated badly

I hated myself
Just so I could love you

I justified the scars
Because I loved the one holding the knife

You said you were afraid to hurt me
Not as sympathy
Not as fear
But as a warning

To this day,
I apologize for letting the younger me
Be hurt the way you hurt me

Why do I care so much in a world that cares so little

I write because no one listens

I wish I could be loved the way I love others

Whose fault is it?
Yours for leaving me
Or mine for believing you never would?

I need to stop asking for love
And start asking for less pain

Stop telling me you love me
Just because I love you

I definitely won the "I love you more" game

It hurts when my voice shows my emotion

Just because it's not said
Doesn't mean it's not felt

You only wanted me
When you had no one else
I wanted you
Because you made me feel
Like I didn't need anyone else

You definitely had your fingers crossed
When you said you loved me

I need to stop begging for you to feel the way I feel

I've been the girl who had all the boys' attention
Or the girl who felt good enough for once
But I've also been the girl who held the blade to her wrist
The girl who hated herself
I've felt the joy
I've felt the sadness
And I've felt the emptiness
So I understand the pain
And I understand the frustration
But nothing will ever feel the same way as when I felt alone

She's beautiful
But she doesn't know it
She has me wrapped around her little finger
And the chase for her will never end
I love every moment I spend loving her
And receiving her love
She's different
And I know I've said it before
And I know things change quickly
But she is
And I know it
She tells me she is here for the long term
And for the first time,
I believe her
I believe someone who says they'll love me forever
I believe someone who shows their love day in and day out
She's here and she's staying
And I never want her to leave

Princes turn to princesses
Fear turns to confidence
And love turns into real love
Futures are less blurry
And possibilities come into focus
Dreams come true with…
Her
She is beauty
She is hope
She is love
She's my wish upon a star
She's my princess charming
She's what I need
Yes, beauty is initially seen on the outside
But she,
She's beautiful inside and out
She's the kind of beautiful that makes you wonder
"How is this possible?"
She's the kind of beautiful that makes people look twice
She's beautiful like the complexity of nature
The awe you feel when you realize your dreams are coming true
She's the beauty that grows the more you know her
She is the definition of beauty
She's beautiful
And I will make it my goal to remind her every single day
Love is beautiful
And I can tell you this:
She's the beauty of love

You treated me so badly
But I masochistically enjoyed it
Your anger cut me deep, but I justified the wounds
And enjoyed every part of it
My blood was on your hands, but you wiped them back onto mine
Everything was my fault, remember?
You were perfect, right?
You *never* did anything wrong
I was the problem even though my hands were clean
You made love seem dreadful, horrible
You tainted love with the wiping of my blood
But you can't be caught red-handed if your hands aren't red

I never imagined myself wishing someone pain or heartbreak
And I guess I can't say I fully want you hurt
But I can tell you this
I can't wish you happiness
And I don't wish you joy
I truly hope no one ever treats you the way you treated me
Because I absolutely hated myself the entire time
Made myself believe that's what love was supposed to be
I do want to thank you
Thank you for ruining my life
Thank you for treating me like shit
And thank you for giving me a final reason to leave
Because if you didn't cheat
I would've never left

You tell me you love me
Tell me how you can't wait for our future to come
"I couldn't do life without you"
"I can't wait to see you"
But that life without me seems to happen suddenly
There is always someone better, right?
Someone prettier, smarter
Someone *closer*
You gushed over me, constantly saying you loved me
But you said it out of convenience
I'm sure when your lips were on hers, you loved her
I'm sure when your fingers slipped into her, she loved you
I thought my love for you would never fade
Until your promises became little white lies

The sunlight hits them perfectly
It simply captures her full beauty
And I spend time lost in them as I get love drunk, intoxicated by
    her elegance
They hold pain, joy, anger
They hold love
They've shed tears of sadness
But grew tears of bliss
A beautiful blue that seems gray until the sun kisses her sweet
    skin
Her soft complexation glistens
I'm in love with her and she will never understand
But her eyes,
God, they're beautiful
God, *she's* beautiful

We should dance in the rain
Hold hands, feel the damp grass beneath our toes
Mother Nature's tears cold on our skin
We should chase the end of the rainbow
Just to realize the happiness is this moment
The moment under the opened skies
We should kiss when it comes down harder
The sweet rain complimenting your soft lips
Our warm breaths mixing in the space between our yearning mouths
We should be kids again
Finding worms
Hoping the rain never stops
We should be in the rain
Me and you
And make the memories last forever
We should kiss in the rain like there is no tomorrow

Let me fall in love with you
Take my hand
And explore the world with you
Let me love you
And show you what love can truly feel like
Let's fall in love like they do in the movies
Make the Hollywood dreams come true
Let me admire you like you put the stars in the sky
As they dance around the moon
So please,
Let me love you
The way you should be
Let's fall in love
And never look back
Let's love like there is no tomorrow
Because there may not be
Let's love through tears of joy
Let's love through tears of anger
Let's love through the pain
Let's love through the awe
Let's love through the wonder
And let me show you
That you are far from unlovable
Let me show you what love can be
And the beauty of it all
So please,
Let's fall in love

I want the slow, foggy mornings
Dragging our feet to get out of bed
I want the sunny days
Dancing in the kitchen, wooden spoons as our microphones
I want the grief and the sorrow
Realizing that life is difficult at times
I want the rainy days that force us to stay inside
Movies and cuddles on the couch
Or going outside and kissing in the rain
I want Christmas mornings
And the late New Year's Eve
I want the making of breakfast for you in bed
I want the soft kisses when I stub a toe
Or when I scrape a knee
I want the whispered "I love yous" when we are dozing off to sleep
And to hear your voice prideful each time you say it
I want the wiping of cheeks when a warm tear is shed
I want the pinky promises we hold dear to our hearts
I want the memories
I want the laughs
I want the cries
I want you
And I want us
Forever and always

About the Author

Author Caitlyn Gehl was born and raised in Horseheads, a small town in Upstate New York. She has enjoyed writing in school, but she found even more joy in writing poems. Expressing her joy, anger, sadness, and love, Caitlyn has loved putting her feelings in writing, and she is finally ready to share those emotions with the world.

Printed in the USA
CPSIA information can be obtained
at www.ICGtesting.com
LVHW040732310324
775939LV00031BA/330